CLIMATE CHANGE
Effects on Seagrass and Marine Life

By Meegan Fourmile

We respect and honour Aboriginal and Torres Strait Islander Elders past, present and future. We acknowledge the stories, traditions and living cultures of Aboriginal and Torres Strait Islander peoples on this land and commit to building a brighter future together.

Library For All Ltd.

Understanding Climate Change

What Science Says About Climate Change

Climate change is caused by the Earth getting too warm too quickly, mostly due to increased pollution, like carbon dioxide. This warming causes changes in the weather and ocean temperatures.

A consequence of climate change has been an increase in dangerous weather and natural hazards.

Plus, climate change has caused a rise in ocean temperatures.

Understanding Climate Change

Indigenous Perspective on Climate Change

Traditionally, Indigenous people are seasonal gatherers, and the weather plays a significant role in the growth and availability of certain flora and fauna. For the Rangers and the community in Yarrabah, there are two seasons: *Gurabuna* is the wet season, and *Guraminya* is the dry season. The timing and duration of these seasons have been changing, which has heavily impacted the plants and animals.

Plants are now flowering at different times, affecting harvests and quality. For example, climate change has caused the black bean tree, a traditional Indigenous food in Yarrabah, to fruit at different times. This has made it difficult to predict the time of harvest. The change in harvest times also affects animals, leading to food instability for fauna.

Impact of Climate Change on Seagrass Ecosystems

Seagrass needs sunlight and relatively clean water in order to survive and grow. However, with changes in our current climate (climate change) it is predicted that severe weather events like cyclones and flooding will become more frequent and more intense.

These events, occurring more often, will physically impact seagrass through removal and burial (cyclones/storms), and also make it harder for seagrass to get enough sunlight (floods) to stay healthy.

Seagrass Ecosystem Changes from Indigenous Perspectives

Traditional owners have been observing the shrinking of seagrass meadows. Sand movement and sediment from floods and cyclones have caused this seagrass decline. Some seagrass meadows regenerate, but many have been covered from sand movement caused from cyclones and flooding.

The increase in storm activity and severity, caused by climate change has led to additional dirt, making the water dirtier/cloudier, directly affecting seagrasses.

Seagrass is the primary source of food for dugongs, and a supplementary source for turtles. Sightings of these animals have declined.

Dugongs and turtles love seagrass, so unhealthy seagrass means they cannot eat.

Effects on Dugongs and Turtles

The Science of Marine Life

If turtles and dugongs cannot find enough food, it is difficult for them to grow, travel and have babies. The effect of climate change on cyclones, storms and floods can make it harder for seagrass to grow, impacting the main food source of dugong and green turtles.

Plastic pollution, boat strikes and fishing also negatively impact dugong and turtle populations.

Effects on Dugongs and Turtles

Because climate change is a relatively new problem, the Rangers believe that dugongs and turtles have not had time to adapt to the changes that have been created in their ecosystem.

The Indigenous Perspective on Marine Life

Dugongs have not adapted to eating different plants, like algae or tougher types of seagrasses that have survived better against climate change. If climate change continues as fast as it is now, we are worried that dugongs will not adapt quickly enough, or change their eating habitats quickly enough to keep up with climate change.

After cyclones, storms and floods, dugongs often have to travel a long way to find healthy seagrass. On the journey, they can starve, and sometimes they die.

Cultural and Ecological Significance of Marine Ecosystem Changes

Declines in seagrass can not only have an impact on dugongs and turtles, it can impact other animals. Seagrass provides a home for smaller marine creatures like prawns and baby fish. Plus, seagrass cleans water, which can remove carbon dioxide from the ocean atmosphere!

Without seagrass, the whole marine environment is less healthy.

Indigenous Perspectives on Marine Ecosystem Changes

Changes that have occurred in Indigenous sea Country over thousands of years have been passed down the generations. Because climate change is a newer problem, there are no known traditional stories of it.

However, the current struggles of seagrasses, turtles and dugongs will be represented in future stories and art. The stories will illustrate how some traditional customs have been threatened by climate change.

For thousands of years, Indigenous people have hunted dugongs, turtles and fish that rely on seagrass. The decline in the ocean's health and the numbers of animals in the ocean have greatly impacted this tradition.

Scientists are still studying how marine life adapts to climate change.

DID YOU KNOW?

Some seagrasses can adjust to different temperatures and grow in warmer water. However, there is a limit.

The temperature of sand can influence the sex of green turtle eggs. Due to climate change, there are currently more females being born than males.

Australia has the largest population of dugongs in the world, with over 100 000!

Seagrass seeds are spread by dugong faeces! This helps to spread genetic diversity.

Marine Science Facts from Indigenous Perspectives

The restoration and protection of marine environments involves Rangers and Indigenous communities who have key knowledge on ways to protect sea Country from climate change. The health of marine life is deeply connected to cultural practices and traditional knowledge.

There are approximately 30 species of seagrass in Australia. Traditional knowledge helps keep them safe.

Other animals that rely on seagrass include fish, crabs, prawns and small invertebrates, like octopuses. They use the seagrass meadows as shelter *and* food. Seagrass meadows can be nursery grounds for some animals before they move out to the big ocean.

DID YOU KNOW?

Animals rely on environmental cues for when to mate and search for food. Because of climate change, these cues are becoming less clear for the animals.

Combating Climate Change

Modern Strategies

Scientists and conservationists are already working to reduce plastic pollution, protect marine habitats and restore damaged habitat. By taking care of wetlands, mangroves, seagrass and reef, the amazing animals that rely on them are also supported.

Traditional Environmental Management

Rangers replant seagrass meadows using biodegradable mats and seagrass snaggers to protect the new seeds in affected areas.

Traditional owners are practising sustainable fishing and rebuilding fish traps, which act as a barrier against large waves.

Marine Protected Areas (MPAs) have been created, limiting human presence and prioritising anti-pollution efforts. Indigenous Rangers monitor the health of habitats and animal populations to then help guide conservationists and scientists with further restoration work.

Photo Credits

Page	Attribution
Cover	Laura Dts/Shutterstock.com
Page 2-3	Photo courtesy of the Queensland Indigenous Land and Sea Ranger Program.
Page 5 (above)	Tammy Walker/iStockphoto.com
Page 5 (below)	Ken Griffiths/Shutterstock.com
Page 6 (above)	Mike Workman/Shutterstock.com
Page 6 (below)	Steven Giles/Shutterstock.com
Page 7	Petr Slezak/Shutterstock.com
Page 8 (above)	(C) Library For All
Page 8 (below)	(C) Library For All
Page 8 (background)	Rich Carey/Shutterstock.com
Page 9	Maryshot/Shutterstock.com
Page 10	Photo courtesy of the Queensland Indigenous Land and Sea Ranger Program.
Page 11	Francisco Glez/Shutterstock.com
Page 12	Nina Milton/Shutterstock.com
Page 13 (above)	rweisswald/Shutterstock.com
Page 13 (below)	James C Farr/Shutterstock.com
Page 14	Photo courtesy of the Queensland Indigenous Land and Sea Ranger Program.
Page 16	Photo courtesy of the Queensland Indigenous Land and Sea Ranger Program.
Page 17	Philip Schubert/Shutterstock.com
Page 18	Photo courtesy of the Queensland Indigenous Land and Sea Ranger Program.
Page 19 (below)	Dr Elizabeth Sinclair/The University of Western Australia
Page 19 (above)	John Carnemolla/Shutterstock.com

You can use these questions to talk about this book with your family, friends and teachers.

What did you learn from this book?

Describe this book in one word. Funny? Scary? Colourful? Interesting?

How did this book make you feel when you finished reading it?

What was your favourite part of this book?

Download the Library For All Reader app from libraryforall.org

Queensland Indigenous Land and Sea Ranger Program

The Queensland Indigenous Land and Sea Ranger Program collaborates with First Nations communities to protect and care for land and sea Country. With over 200 rangers, the program shares cultural knowledge, engages in community education, and leads youth programs like the Junior Ranger initiative, fostering a strong connection to Country and Culture.

Meegan Fourmile is a GMYPPBC Ranger from the Yarrabah community.

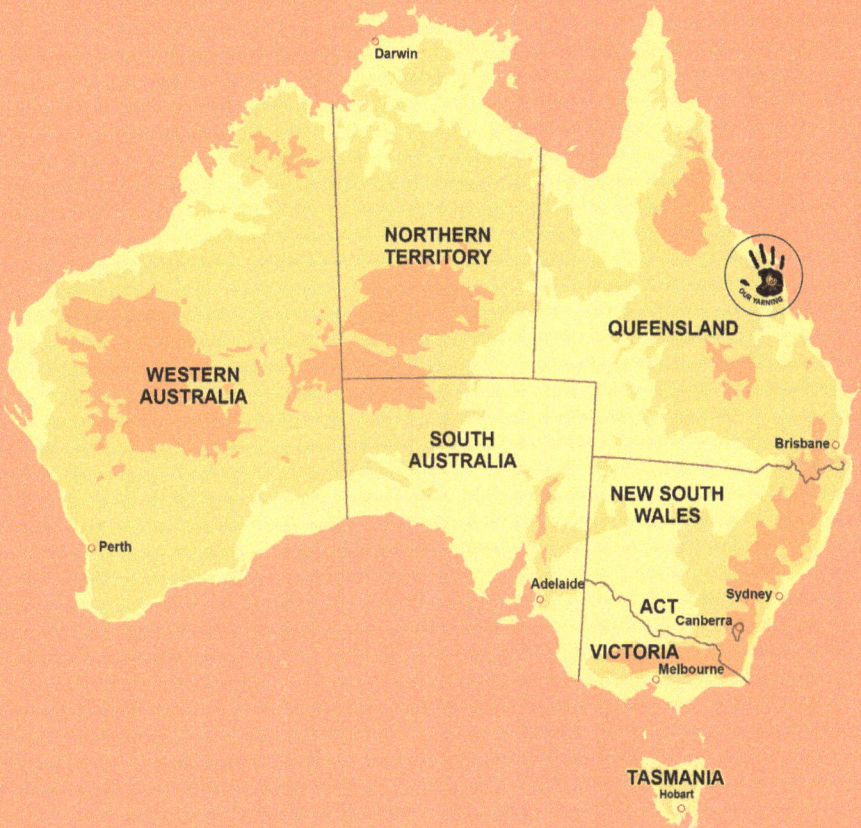

Our Yarning

The Our Yarning collection aligns with the Australian Curriculum through the Cross-Curriculum Priorities — Aboriginal and Torres Strait Islander Histories and Cultures. The collection provides an authentic opportunity for learning and embedding Aboriginal and Torres Strait Islander perspectives because it is written by Aboriginal and Torres Strait Islander people.

We know that children learn better, and enjoy reading more, when they see themselves in the stories, characters and illustrations of the books they read.

To download the app, visit the Google Play Store or Apple Store and search 'Our Yarning'.

libraryforall.org

You're reading Upper Primary

Learner – Beginner readers

Start your reading journey with short words, big ideas and plenty of pictures.

Level 1 – Rising readers

Raise your reading level with more words, simple sentences and exciting images.

Level 2 – Eager readers

Enjoy your reading time with familiar words, but complex sentences.

Level 3 – Progressing readers

Develop your reading skills with creative stories and some challenging vocabulary.

Level 4 – Fluent readers

Step up your reading skills with playful narratives, new words and fun facts.

Middle Primary – Curious readers

Discover your world through science and stories.

Upper Primary – Adventurous readers

Explore your world through science and stories.

Climate Change: Effects on Seagrass and Marine Life

First published 2024

Published by Library For All Ltd
Email: info@libraryforall.org
URL: libraryforall.org

This project was delivered with the support of QBE under the Community Ready partnership.

Community Ready

This book was made possible with the support of the Queensland Indigenous Land and Sea Ranger Program to support educational outcomes for children in Australia by learning from Indigenous knowledge and stewardship of Country. To learn more, visit https://www.qld.gov.au/environment/plants-animals/conservation/community/land-sea-rangers/locations.

Queensland Indigenous Land and Sea Rangers

Queensland Government

Our Yarning logo design by Jason Lee, Bidjipidji Art

Climate Change: Effects on Seagrass and Marine Life
Fourmile, Meegan
ISBN: 978-1-923207-25-7
SKU04430